oasis
a year in the life

UFO Music Ltd 18 Hanway Street London W1P 9DD England
Telephone: 0171 636 1281   Fax: 0171 636 0738

First published in Great Britain 1997

ISBN 1-873884-76-1

Printed by Lawrence-Allen, Weston-Super-Mare
Designed by Mike Edgar at UFO Music Ltd

ACKNOWLEDGEMENTS
FRONT COVER © DAVE CHANCELLOR/ALPHA

© ALL ACTION 57
© JUSTIN THOMAS/ALL ACTION 55, 56
© EAMONN CLARKE/ALL ACTION 62, 63

© ALPHA London 4, 14, 20, 50
© JOHN LEYTON/ALPHA 22
© DAVE PARKER/ALPHA 24, 33, 34, 36
© RICHARD CHAMBURY/ALPHA 29, 38, 44, 48, 64 (second from top)
© DAVE BENETT/ALPHA 34, 46, 47, 52, 54
© MARK ALLAN/ALPHA 42, 64 (middle)
© DAVE CHANCELLOR/ALPHA 58, 59, 60

© ILPO MUSTO/LFI 13
© KEVIN MAZUR/LFI 14, 28, 64 (bottom)
© COLIN STREATER/LFI 16
© JOE HUGHES/LFI 26
© DAVID FISHER/LFI 40

© PATRICK FORD/REDFERNS 8, 10
© PHIL SMITH/REDFERNS 12
© MARC MARNIE//REDFERNS 15
© ROBERTA PARKIN//REDFERNS 16
© JADRANKA KRSTESKE/REDFERNS 18, 64 (top)

© UFO Music Ltd 6, 7, 51, 64

With special thanks to the following publications:
*The Daily Star, The Evening Standard, The Guardian, The Mirror, The Sunday Mirror, The
News of the World, The Sun, The Times, The New York Times, Melody Maker, NME,
Mojo, Loaded, Select, Q, Kerrang!, Here!* and *The Face*

oasis

a year
in the life

Susan Wilson

When 1996 began, Oasis were sitting on top of the world. They had two multi-million selling albums behind them, a globeful of dedicated fans and notorious celebrity status. They were absolutely massive as a band, infamous as characters, and nearly as famous as The Beatles. What more could Oasis possibly want?

Well for one, Noel Gallagher, the band's songwriter and guitarist wasn't satisfied. At the start of the year, speaking with Phil Sutcliffe for *Q* magazine, he recalled a lot about his background and family life and reflected on the ways in which success had affected him and his relationships with the rest of Oasis. Without delving too much into the personal side, he admitted that the main difference was financial. Being the songwriter, Noel claimed publishing royalties, and unlike Pulp's Jarvis Cocker, he refused to split any of the money with the other band members. Most musicians make their money from publishing, and those who don't actually write songs can't expect to earn an enormous wage unless their band is absolutely huge. Fortunately for everyone in Oasis apart from Noel, the band were absolutely huge, although Noel hinted slightly at some conflict arising from the money imbalance. His justification however, was that he was the one who sat up for 48 hours thinking up tunes, making his girlfriend suffer; he was the one who had to come up with the goods every time an album was due. He deserved the money.

In the spring of 1996 Oasis were busy cracking America, succeeding where almost all of the other British 'Britpop' acts had failed. Other than Bush, who had positively exploded Stateside, through playing the kind of powerful guitar rock Americans hankered after since the day of The Pixies and Nirvana, and Radiohead, whose sheer genius could only be disputed by the foolish and the tasteless, no British band had truly ignited the American imagination – or the weight of the American wallet. Elastica had won themselves the patronage of Courtney Love and enjoyed a stint on the Lollapalooza tour, as had The Verve and The Charlatans, and Lush had made inroads with their hit singles 'Single Girl', and 'Ladykiller', but Blur, Suede, and all the other bands who were supposedly reinventing swinging London for the nineties couldn't compete with the likes of Alanis Morrisette and Pearl Jam.

Oasis' big break came with the release of 'Wonderwall' (which also reached number one in Britain). Perfect for radio play, it was a powerful song which avoided the ballad tag by bearing the unmistakeable imprint of the brash Mancunians, but its anthemic quality grabbed America by the throat. *(What's The Story) Morning Glory* rocketed to the top of the US album charts, and the band disappeared across the Atlantic to play a succession of sold-out tours.

Oasis' American success had begun even before they were contractually signed (although they were as good as hooked

up with Creation Records), when their soon-to-be label boss, Alan McGee, went to the major labels looking for a US deal. Demo tape in hand, he managed to court the big names, and together with British born Richard Griffiths, head of Epic in America, David Massey, also British, head of A&R for Epic US, and the band's manager, Marcus Russell, he got the band a decent Stateside deal.

Massey first saw the band at London's Powerhaus venue, then a small space in Islington. Immediately he recognised a quality which excited him.

"It was at a time when UK bands were cold as ice in the US," he told Steve Malins of *Q* magazine. "And there was some cynicism in the company when we signed them – but we were already convinced."

A strategic plan of action was devised by the pair at Epic. *Definitely Maybe*, the band's debut album, was released in the US in 1995, just after it had been issued in Britain. Knowing that a second album was on its way, the idea was to use the first as an introductory measure. Sales figures weren't of prime importance at this stage. The aim was to build the band a following, and then unleash all the forces upon the public at a later date.

To begin with, Oasis toured round all the dingy clubs,

returning regularly to maintain and increase the fanbase. 'Live Forever' was released and sold about 50,000, and 'Morning Glory' came next, shifting about 250,000. 'Wonderwall' was saved for a while, because Epic wanted America to see Oasis' rock side before crossing the band over to pop radio, but when 'Wonderwall' was released, it was a huge hit.

The band's second album, *(What's The Story) Morning Glory?* broke into the US Top Five, and was selling at the rate of 100,000 copies per week, proving that the products of Britpop could export their music, as long as they weren't too parochial (like Blur and Pulp, both of whom were lost in the cultural translation), too ironic, or too blasé. Cracking America entails touring, touring and more touring, and Oasis had the discipline and the tenacity to do it. In just two years they toured the States three times. Their attitude also had plenty to do with their success.

"They unashamedly want to be successful at a time when a lot of American bands have been quite deliberately doing what they can to try and limit their success and be very much the anti-hero," explained Richard Griffiths to *Q*. "The Gallagher brothers have shaken the Americans up a bit – and they get away with it because they're incredible. If Damon whatsisname came out and said all that 'wanna be a star' stuff, it wouldn't work. I loved it when he said he didn't really care about America. What bullshit. Anybody in this business cares about America."

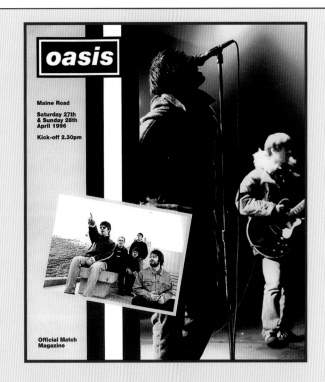

ABOVE *The official programme for Oasis at Maine Road, Manchester City's football ground. April 27 and 28, 1996.*

LEFT *Noel with his famous Union Jack guitar at Maine Road.*

On tour with the band in America in March, photographer Jill Furmanovsky documented as much as she could, letting *Mojo* magazine reproduce some of her images. She also expressed some of her thoughts on the relationship between Oasis and their Stateside fans.

"To some extent I think America is a bit baffled by Oasis," she said. "Noel's acoustic set for example – the band just stop, it looks like the show may be finished, and then the stool comes on. During the gig in Rhode Island, when he was doing his solo bit, the audience was vibed up to rock and roll. This boot came sailing out of the crowd and hit him on the side of his head and then fell onto his guitar. Noel just walked off, and Liam came back on and went absolutely berserk, screaming at the audience that Noel was a great songwriter and that they should pay him more respect. I think it was just simply that American audiences haven't quite twigged that Oasis aren't like the local bands who were supporting them – rock bands who still get down on their knees and throw guitar poses.

"To some degree their presentation has an element of menace, Liam seems as much influenced by John Lydon as John Lennon, and Noel is almost folksy – it's an odd combination for a US audience."

Jill took photos of Liam sleeping on the bus, of Noel on stage at a ski resort outside New York, where he played in sub zero

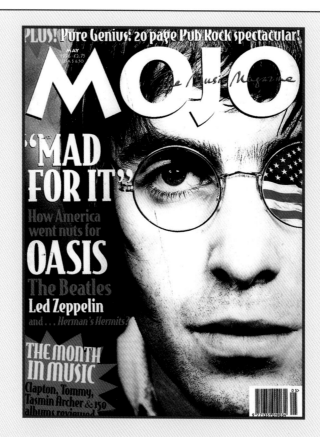

ABOVE *MOJO Magazine, May 1996.*

LEFT *Liam at Maine Road.*

temperatures and had to give up before his fingers froze to his guitar, of the band's beloved crew with whom she noted they shared an unusual sense of camaraderie, and of general backstage and on stage and soundcheck activity. Soundchecks were the best musically she decided, because that's when Noel made up new tunes. And she noticed the ever swelling ranks of female fans who'd wait for hours in the freezing cold for a glimpse of their heroes. Ironically, since he was the one least likely to oblige the record company, Liam was the most obliging when it came to autographs and posing for pictures with the fans, even though they found him a bit scarey on the strength of his bad boy reputation. While Noel was the consummate professional, Liam was still irreverent, and while that was annoying for his label and people working with him (apparently he screwed up one of Jill's photo sessions by sleeping through it), it was, Jill acknowledged, his way of staying sane amidst the growing chaos around him.

Oasis' appeal wasn't always fully accepted by Americans however. Pondering over the band, writer Dave Marsh couldn't really make head nor tail of them in his article for *Mojo*. He was completely confounded by their lack of passion during performance, and found himself more or less unmoved by them. He thought them to be utterly calculated, although he conceded that they had great songs. Yet ultimately, he decided they were something of an empty experience. Maybe, for Marsh at least, something did get lost in the translation after all.

ABOVE *Liam with his familiar tambourine at Loch Lomond.*

LEFT *The whole gang together before their Scottish shows.*

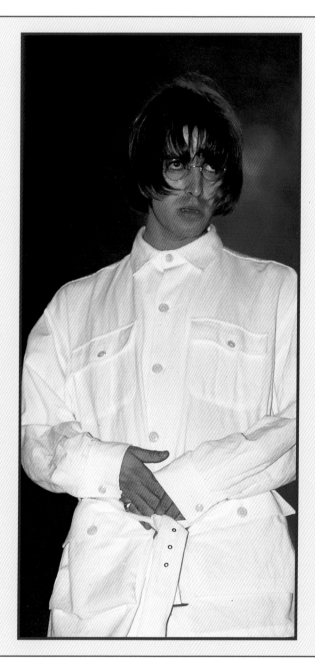

In the summer of 1996, Oasis returned to Britain to play two enormous outdoor gigs. With Glastonbury having been called off, Britain wasn't short on festival action, as V96, T -in The Park, Phoenix and Reading, plus the Tribal Gathering and a host of other small events took place. But Oasis wanted to give their fans something really special, so they ambitiously scheduled in concerts at Knebworth and Loch Lomond.

Both events were absolutely massive. The usual controversy ensued after the dates were announced, with local councils expressing concern about the size of the shows and the possible accompanying problems, but in the end everything went ahead and thousands upon thousands of Oasis fans were given the days of their lives. The press went into overdrive, with every music paper worth its salt detailing both gigs, snapping shots of every celebrity worth mentioning who showed up, and reporting on the frenzied crowd action.

At Knebworth Liam threw a strop after squabbling with Patsy Kensit, the actress who had finally succeeded in catching one of the world's most desirable men. The pair were photographed during their bickering on the back of a buggy which was transporting Liam to the main stage. His bad mood resulted in him bellowing abuse at the crowd as the vehicle barged through. Fortunately the actual concert went without a hitch, but Patsy's 'Yoko' reputation hadn't been done any favours.

ABOVE & LEFT *Liam and Noel enjoying two sell-out shows at Knebworth Park.*

Patsy Kensit had a track record of hobnobbing with rich and famous rock stars. Beginning with one of Brother Beyond, moving on to marry one of Big Audio Dynamite, dumping him for Simple Minds singer Jim Kerr – once Simple Minds took off in America, noted the cynics – and eventually dumping him for the far more rich and famous, and younger and better looking Gallagher boy, she had launched a full scale chase on Liam in 1995, managing to fend off many other starstruck, lust-hungry bit-part actresses like Amanda de Cadanet and tabloid queen Paula Yates. According to Patsy, she already had a crush on Liam, and managed to meet him backstage after a show. She didn't think he'd like her, but he evidently did, and they arranged a date. Apparently the two fell in love during a holiday to Anguilla, three months after Oasis played at Maine Road, and before long, they were frequently snapped together pouting, done up in expensive designer outfits.

Rumours of Patsy being pregnant began to fly after she flew out to visit Liam while Oasis were busy touring America, and more rumours of his fooling around (he'd never made a secret of his sexual appetite, which was as healthy as his appetite for fame, drugs, attention and all the other trappings of the rock'n'roll lifestyle) and gossip about the couple's continually stormy relationship started to surface. Nevertheless, by the end of the year they were being hailed as rock's most glamorous couple. Patsy appeared on the covers of *The Face* and *Vogue* (which also featured shots of the pair kissing

ABOVE *The official programme for Oasis at Knebworth Park. August 10 and 11, 1996.*

inside) and it seemed that her latest rock liaison wasn't merely giving her career a serious boost – it was also serious.

After their two massive summer highlights in Britain, Oasis were due to return to America where they had another heavy touring schedule to fulfil. But this time, all hell broke loose.

Just a week before Oasis were due to fly to America for a tour, Liam pulled out of a secret gig which had been due to take place on Friday, August 23rd at the Royal Festival Hall for the recording of an MTV 'Unplugged' episode. The unofficial story was that Liam and Noel had fallen out during or just after rehearsals although laryngitis was the reason given. On the evening this latter excuse looked unlikely as the singer sat in the box with Patsy Kensit and watched his brother take up vocals as well as guitar, drinking and smoking throughout the performance.

MTV were less than happy at Liam's refusal to sing for their 'Unplugged' session in London, and considered forgoing the whole show which was scheduled to be aired in the US on October 14th. They were also worried about using the band for the showcase slot in their live Video Music Awards which were due to take place in New York about a week after the tour fiasco. Apparently Oasis were just too unpredictable for MTV to be comfortable with.

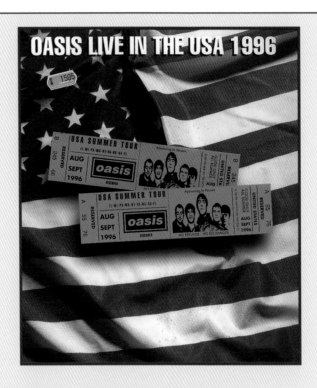

ABOVE *The official programme for the ill-fated US tour.*

To make matters worse, Liam Gallagher pulled out of Oasis' American tour 15 minutes before he was due to leave, and instead stayed home to be with his now fianceé Patsy. The tabloid press went ballistic, and the news even found its way onto television, with reporters camped outside the couple's home in St John's Wood, north London. Rumours about the demise of Oasis began to fly, and everyone was sniffing for the truth behind the drama.

On August 28th, *The Daily Mirror* ran a front page story about Patsy sending Liam into therapy. Apparently he was seeing Adam Jukes, who blamed Liam's problems on his unstable relationship with his brother, Noel, as well as the pressures of fame. According to a 'friend' of Liam's, Patsy had been having terrible rows with her boyfriend in March when the band were in Ireland, and it was this which made her decide that he needed to see someone outside of the band and his family to discuss his problems. Apparently he made contact with Jukes at this point.

Jukes told *Here!* magazine how he didn't even realise who Liam was, although once he began to read background notes, it soon became clear that his band were huge. He attributed Liam's difficulties to sibling rivalry, mainly jealousy of Noel's songwriting ability, and his drink and drugs problems he blamed on Liam's loss of identity. There was also his childhood background. When Liam was 12, his mother Peggy

LEFT & BELOW *The Mirror newspaper, Wednesday August 28, 1996.*

oasis *a year in the life*

took him and brothers Noel and Paul away from their father, Tommy, and set up home in Burnage, Manchester. Tommy had been a drinker and prone to violence, frequently delivering beatings to his family, and while the split devastated Liam, he wasn't glad to see the back of his dad.

"If I ever see him again, I'll slit his throat," he said.

The Gallagher boys were given a strict Catholic upbringing, and learned to respect their mother. As adults they were still terrified of upsetting her, and didn't like her to see them after they'd been drinking.

In an interview with the *Sunday Mirror*, Paul, the oldest Gallagher, blamed Liam's aggressive behaviour on his father's violence, and pointed out that Noel expressed his sadness through his songs.

"He helped make us the people we are today," he said.

While the press was going into overdrive, scrutinising the Gallaghers' home life and family background, speculation about Liam's future reached fever pitch on Thursday 29th August, when he departed for Detroit city in America after all. Despite his claims earlier that week that he wasn't going to "sing for fucking Yanks" while he had more pressing matters to attend to, such as house-hunting, he travelled to Heathrow

LEFT & BELOW *The Sunday Mirror, Sunday September 8, 1996.*

in a chauffeur-driven Mercedes with two bodyguards and took a flight to Chicago, yelling, "You're all wankers. I hate you fucking lot," at the waiting journalists and photographers who'd plagued him for the past few days. "You're always asking me to do things. I'm not a supermodel."

Liam's explanation for not going to the States was that again he'd been suffering from laryngitis, not psychological traumas, and he'd stayed home until the doctors had given him the all clear. He'd also been helping Patsy hunt for a new house, as the one in which they currently lived had been sold and they were given precisely one week to vacate the premises.

"We had to find a house, I had to move," he explained. "The thousands of fans can wait. I don't care. I'm not going on the street."

Defending Patsy to the press, many of whom had blamed her for trying to break up the band, he said that he loved her and that she would never stop him doing anything. As for Noel, he insisted there was no problem between him and his older brother, and that the two had spoken on the phone and everything was cool.

Over in the States, Noel admitted that Oasis had not been doing so well without their frontman. Many fans had felt let

ABOVE *The Times, Thursday August 29, 1996.*

LEFT *Liam, at Heathrow, finally leaves for the US.*

down and upset at seeing their heroes without the lead singer, and the band were definitely struggling without him. However, Noel also added that he would always stand by Liam in his moment of "personal crisis".

With Liam gone, Patsy found herself having to fend off the reporters single-handedly. Questions were still flying around about his reputed visits to Jukes, but Patsy was determined to lay them to rest.

"I know we are famous," she said outside her home in St John's Wood, "but I have never seen such a load of lies printed in such a short space of time.

"I never tell Liam what to do. The therapy is a lie, the drug problem is a lie. There will be legal action, we are not happy."

Before leaving for a shopping trip, she announced that she would be flying out to join her boyfriend with Meg Matthews, Noel's girlfriend.

Later in the year, clarifying her own and Liam's positions to *The Face* (Patsy had requested that the magazine interview her), Patsy pointed out that she had been made to feel like "the evilest woman in Britain" about the whole affair, and that she'd nearly fled to Ireland but Liam had stopped her because he needed her at home. As Liam pointed out, Noel's girlfriend

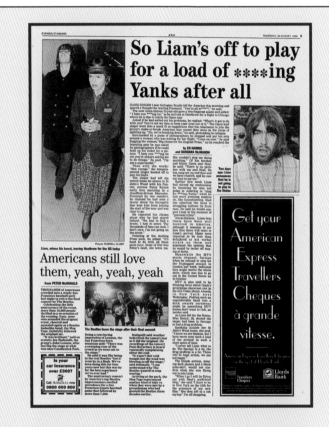

ABOVE *The London Evening Standard, Thursday August 29, 1996.*

Meg didn't receive such unwelcome treatment, but then Meg wasn't a public figure with a dubious career record and a history of rock star boyfriends and husbands. Patsy was a sitting duck for the tabloids and the music press alike, much in the same way as Courtney Love had been with the whole Kurt Cobain/Nirvana fiasco. Patsy took the brunt of everyone's anger and disappointment, finding herself the scapegoat of the situation. *The Daily Mirror* hadn't helped. It was they who'd reported that Patsy was responsible for sending Liam into therapy, thereby enabling others to point the finger at an already unpopular personality. And as it turned out, they didn't appear to have any solid evidence as to whether or not Liam had actually seen a therapist.

When questioned by the *Daily Mirror,* the therapist implied by the press reports, Adam Jukes, refused to confirm or deny that he was treating Liam, and lawyers representing the singer firmly denied that he was suffering from any psychological problems. A spokesman for Creation, the band's record label, also denied any therapist stories to the music press.

Whether Liam was suffering mentally or not, it soon became clear that Oasis were in trouble – again. The American tour seemed to have settled down and things were going smoothly until September 4th when the MTV Awards took place at the New York Radio City Music Hall. MTV had already expressed concern at having the volatile Mancunians appear at this event,

ABOVE *Liam with his then soon-to-be wife Patsy, and bodyguard.*

RIGHT & BELOW *Daily Star, Friday September 13,*

1996.

and it turned out that their nervous predictions proved right. During the band's rendition of 'Champagne Supernova', Liam swore, spat and altered the lyrics to 'champagne supernova up yer bum!' He also knocked over the microphone stand and tossed a can of beer into the air. The press were waiting and flung themselves into another field day at the band's expense.

A few more gigs were played, but the pressures were evidently taking their toll, and the biggest news came when Noel flew home from America, leaving behind a tattered trail. Two thirds of the way through their 17-date tour of the States, internal difficulties had halted band activities, and this time it looked really serious.

As he stepped off Concorde, flanked by three bodyguards and three airport staff, looking tired and fed up, Noel refused to grant any journalists interviews. He didn't even comment on the situation to the awaiting army of 200 fans and press people. Instead, he was simply led to a blacked-out vehicle and driven off to meet his girlfriend, Meg. One Heathrow official told *The Sun*, "He looked out of it. There were none of the outrageous or vulgar antics we've come to expect. If that was anything to go by, he's clearly had enough of Oasis and everything that goes with it."

Liam and the rest of the band flew into Gatwick airport on the day after Noel had arrived back in Britain. None of their party were prepared to comment on what had happened either.

ABOVE *The London Evening Standard, Thursday September 12, 1996.*

RIGHT & BELOW *The Sun, Friday September 13, 1996.*

The story, as reported by the British tabloids who first broke the news, was that Oasis had actually broken up. The decision was made after a five hour summit meeting at the band's hotel in Charlotte, North Carolina, just prior to a show. Liam and Noel apparently had a massive argument which left Liam very distraught and in tears. The reasons for the split were said to be the continually volatile and fiery relationship between the Gallagher brothers, and, this time, the poor reception the band had endured at the hands of the American music critics. The Charlotte show was allegedly originally supposed to take place at the 12,000 capacity Independence Arena, but was downgraded to the 2,500 capacity Hornets Training Facility after ticket sales had slowed up. Noel allegedly declared that he was fed up with "touring shitholes" and refused to go ahead with the show. The band's press officer, Johnny Hopkins, later denied this, insisting that the Hornets Facility had been scheduled in all along, but whatever the truth, Noel was not a happy man. He was also becoming increasingly fed up with his younger brother's heavy drinking and irresponsible behaviour, resented Liam's sex symbol status, and had already announced that the main reason Oasis had minders was to keep him and his brother apart.

Liam, meanwhile, was said to be very homesick, missing Patsy and his family, and finding the pressures of fame difficult to cope with – just as the press had previously reported when he failed to leave the country initially with Oasis

ABOVE *The Sun, Friday September 13, 1996.*

at the beginning of the American tour. Reputedly he'd been telephoning Peggy, his mother, in a distressed state, saying that things were going badly on the tour and that the band were constantly at each other's throats. Apparently at their show in Jones Beach, New York, Noel had turned up his guitar and drowned out all of Liam's in-between-song banter, and at the aftershow the brothers had a huge argument which surprised even those familiar with their fights.

Ian Robertson, the man who tour-managed Oasis before Margaret Mouzakitis took over, and also author of *Oasis: What's The Story*, told *The Sun*, "The boys' relationship is vicious, angry and full of love and hate. If they weren't brothers, Noel would have sacked Liam long ago."

Creation Records, Oasis' record label, issued a press statement holding personnel problems responsible for this latest situation.

"Oasis have hit internal differences on their ninth tour of America which has resulted in the tour being pulled two-thirds of the way through. It is unlikely that immediate touring commitments will be fulfilled," the statement read, while, on Friday September 13th, a spokesman for the label added, "As far as we know, the band and their instruments are in Atlanta. If it [the show] is cancelled, it will be a disappointment but it's just another day in rock'n'roll."

Johnny Hopkins, the band's press officer who worked for them at Creation told *The Sun*, "The American tour is off and the future of Oasis is unknown. It's open ended. It is too early to say if the split is permanent. We just don't know."

The *NME* reported Hopkins as saying, "No one knows what's going on apart from Liam and Noel, so it's pointless saying anything yet. It'll all come out in the wash."

Patsy Kensit, who found herself being blamed again by certain factions for this latest development, spoke from Los Angeles where she was working on a movie project.

"I knew nothing about it until my management office in London rang me. I am as mystified as everyone else. At the moment Liam has no plans to come here."

Jean Wagner, director of marketing and public relations at the Nissan Pavilion, Bristow, Virginia, where Oasis played their final US gig on September 10th, hadn't noticed any problems with the band. She didn't detect any unrest and she was very shocked to hear the news of their departure.

"We had about 12,000 people here and the gig went very well," she told the *NME*. "The crowds were screaming for them. They loved it. I saw the soundcheck and was with them during the day and they seemed to be getting on very well. They were

goofing around and talking and were getting along just fine. I didn't see any signs of strife or problems at all."

By the time the band reached Charlotte, the situation was very different indeed. Jon Percival, the venue manager, was quoted as saying, "We received a statement saying 'Due to unforeseen circumstances, the concert has been cancelled and will not be rescheduled.'"

Ken Johnson, the local pop critic at the *Charlotte Observer* told the *NME*, "Oasis didn't even bother turning up for soundcheck and only let the promoter Marc Farha know at about 6pm that they weren't going to play, so he had to put the word out pretty quickly, but some fans still turned up."

Some of those fans had driven 1,000 miles for the event, and were understandably upset at the disappointment. They'd only had ten minutes' notice that the gig was cancelled, and were waiting for the support act to play when they were told that "in-fighting" had stopped the main act from appearing.

In Atlanta, where the band were due to appear at the Omni on Friday September 13th, 7,000 out of 7,500 tickets had already sold by the time the band had imploded, promoters were unsure as to whether the gig would go ahead or not as members of Oasis were thought to be on their way to the venue. But it was obvious that nothing could go ahead without Noel.

Wallis Barr of Landmark Entertainment, who was promoting the Omni show, told *Melody Maker*, "The promoter of the Charlotte, North Carolina date, called me at 6pm on Wednesday afternoon to tell me the problems that he was having, and from that, I got prepared for what potentially would happen to me. The show was officially cancelled at 4pm on Thursday.

"The Omni is 16,000 seats but we were set up in a 7,500 seat half-house configuration.

"The band is going to reimburse us all out of pocket expenses. That's probably around $20,000. We've started giving refunds via Ticketmaster. I'm sure all the other promoters are as disappointed as us, but if they get their money, they can't be too upset.

"I really don't think this will hurt Oasis in America. You know, the quality of their music will stand for itself and I'm sure the fans are disappointed but I think it's just a bump on the road that they can easily overcome. I think they have the potential to be as big here as they are in the UK.

"I would absolutely work with them again. I'd promote their whole tour here."

Promoters in Florida, Georgia, and elsewhere made it clear that they would be expecting some sort of financial

compensation from the departed British superstars as they were legally obliged to return all tickets. A lawsuit against Epic, Oasis' American label, looked imminent.

According to the *NME*, it wasn't just poor ticket sales which were holding up Oasis in America. Crowd responses hadn't been all they could have been, and the press were far less charitable than their British counterparts. Echoing Dave Marsh's thoughts in *Mojo*, *The New York Times* observed that 'Few bands put out as little and expect as much."

There was no official statement concerning the band's break-up in the *NME*, although the paper did quote Noel on the tensions between him and his younger brother. Speaking on Radio 1's *Evening Session*, he'd said; "We have fights where we call each other all the names under the sun, but it doesn't mean anything. At the end of the day we'd all die for each other. They're my brothers and I'd never give them up for anything. We've had to grow up in public."

The paper also reminded its readers of Noel's previous walkout on his band. In October 1994, after a disastrous show at the Whiskey A Go Go in Los Angeles, the guitarist helped himself to $800 of the tour money and disappeared for five days, forcing the cancellation of shows in Austin, Dallas, Kansas and Missouri. He ended up in Las Vegas and San Francisco, before setting off for the airport to fly back to England. On his way, he opened a copy of *Melody Maker* and noticed an advertisement for a string of sold-out Oasis dates. Needless to say, this prompted him to return to his band, although when he did rejoin them, he told them that they had to quit partying or lose him.

Concluding their report, the *NME* stated that while there were some who believed this latest fracas to be permanent in its effect, with Noel having sorted himself out a £10 million solo deal with Sony, others maintained that the band would continue and that they would be going ahead with plans to record a third album.

Melody Maker had a slightly different version of the tale. News editor Carol Clerk reprinted a statement from Ignition, the band's management, declaring that "Oasis have all arrived back in England. Noel and Liam are spending time together and getting over jet-lag. Unfortunately, the band will not be touring in the foreseeable future, but in every other aspect, Oasis will continue to exist and function as a band."

Clerk maintained that despite this statement, things were not at all clear for Oasis' future, except it now looked as if they were determined to find a way to work together. She traced the band's troubles back to the MTV Royal Festival Hall show, which Liam had stormed out of at the last minute. And indeed, this was the starting point for the press hysteria which built to a crescendo when the 'Oasis split' story broke.

Looking back over Oasis' chequered history in America, Clerk drew attention to the fact that the Mancunians had always had trouble with the country. There was Noel's previous disappearance, there was the incident in 1995 when Liam was hit by a metal-framed pair of glasses on stage in Indianapolis, and cut the show short. And there was another show in Grand Rapids where Liam's voice let him down and Noel had to take his place for the rest of the songs. So was this latest drama really the worst to date, or was it simply that the mainstream media, who'd never really bothered reporting on Oasis before 1996, had got on board and inflated every detail to bursting point?

"This crisis has been the most publicised," said Johnny Hopkins when questioned by Clerk. "This so-called crisis has been blown out of all proportion. The band are still very much a band. It was funny to watch the media writing the band's obituary one day and having to backtrack frantically the next. Oasis never did split up, and by implication, they haven't been saved by any newspapers."

Hopkins' last comment was referring to *The Sun*, the first of the tabloids to scream about Oasis splitting up. The day after their sensational story, they'd run the headline, "*The Sun* saves Oasis" claiming that their paper had glued the band back together because "our scoop triggered a massive wave of worldwide support for Britain's No 1 group".

ABOVE *The Times, Friday September 13, 1996.*

LEFT *Noel Gallagher meets and performs with Burt Bacharach at London's Festival Hall during rumours of an Oasis split.*

ABOVE *News of the World, Sunday*
November 10, 1996.

Attempting to get to the bottom of what had actually occurred in Charlotte, Clerk tried to get Hopkins to proffer some more information, but he refused on the basis that any details should come straight from the mouths of Liam or Noel. He did, however, refute any allegations concerning punch-ups between the brothers, and he also denied that Liam fled any of the arguments in tears.

"Liam wasn't in tears and there was certainly no fight," he insisted.

Nevertheless, as Clerk rightly pointed out, something had gone on in Charlotte. And while she could only speculate, she did run through a list of possibilities which might have contributed to the band's unhappiness.

First of all was the fact that the American tour wasn't going too well. As other papers had noted, venues were either modest, or being scaled down to size, ticket sales weren't exactly phenomenal, and crowd responses were less than satisfactory. Hopkins leapt to the band's defence.

"That's not true at all," he told Clerk. "Most of the shows were sold out, and all were extremely well received by the audiences and the media. I'd say that the band in New York were the best I've ever seen them. Other people who have seen them before were saying the same thing about Boston and Washington.

LEFT & BELOW *News of the World, Sunday November 10, 1996. Just when you thought things couldn't get much worse Liam assaults a reporter.*

"I'd say the remaining gigs (the ones they called off) were all close to selling out, and they probably would have on the day.

"They were playing to audiences of around 12,000 bar the last few dates which were slightly smaller because, essentially, they were in virgin territory. That's why this mad story has arisen, that the tour had been scaled down. It hadn't been at all."

Secondly, Oasis were said to simply be fed up with touring the States. Going back over there again so soon after Knebworth strained band relations, undermined their confidence and resulted in the band imploding. Manager Marcus Russell admitted that it was "one tour too many" according to Clerk, who also indicated that while the band were already under pressure, the tabloid attention no doubt made everything far worse. Even the Gallaghers' mother, Peggy, requested that her sons be left to their own devices.

Reading a statement from her doorstep, a representative for Peggy said she was "pleased that they're not splitting up. She didn't think they would for one moment split up and she just wishes that they're left alone to let them sort themselves out."

Amazingly, once the Gallaghers were back on British turf, no attempts were made to trace them. Liam and Noel left London for a secret location where they were attempting to sort out their differences while the others travelled elsewhere.

ABOVE *Oasis picking more awards up at The Brits '97.*

ABOVE *Noel with his then soon-to-be wife Meg Matthews.*

"Noel and Liam got together to hang out," Hopkins told Clerk. "They're on good terms – yeah, totally. They're mad for it. Of course they're friends. They're staying together and getting over the jet-lag, just chatting away."

With all tours cancelled for the immediate future, the question of whether the band would remain only a studio act arose.

"It's happened before with bands," said Hopkins. "It's too early to say if that will be the case. I think they all love playing live, they all love the response of the crowd, but the experience of touring is the bit they don't enjoy."

And what about *The Daily Star's* report that Liam was intending to make a solo album?

"It's not a sudden thing. Liam's always written songs. Liam and Bonehead wrote 'Take Me', which has been talked about in the past. They all write songs. But there are no plans for a solo album because Oasis are very much a happening thing, and they certainly will be for a good long time to come."

At this stage of the proceedings, the band were facing financial problems with all the money they owed from the cancellation of the tour. Hopkins didn't even bother to comment on the amounts and even Robertson Taylor, the band's insurance agents admitted to Clerk that they were "in the dark like everybody else".

Eventually everything worked out. Oasis survived the worst tabloid storm any band has had to weather, and came out of it completely intact. As Noel had pointed out the previous year, you had to be prepared to go through the mill if you wanted to make it.

"The worst thing to do would be to give up and say, 'I've lost it, I'm going to go and run a trout farm, '" he told *Loaded* magazine in October, 1995. "I'd just keep going, me. You take it out on your girlfriend or the band or your mates, but that's part of being in a group of people or in a relationship. And you shouldn't do it. And you know you shouldn't do it, but that's just part of human nature. The test is, whether the people you take it out on are still there in the end."

For Liam and Noel, two of the longest-suffering individuals, who were both still there in the end, were their girlfriends, Patsy Kensit and Meg Matthews. Meg, an employee of Creation Records who'd formerly had her own company which had unfortunately gone bust, was the subject of 'Wonderwall', Oasis' biggest hit. She shared a flat in Camden with Noel, and was often photographed on shopping sprees with him, loaded down with Prada and Versace bags.

Once Liam had become engaged to Patsy, the same question was levied at Noel, although in an interview with *Select's* Andrew Perry on the day of the Knebworth gig, August 11th, 1996, the guitarist denied that marriage was for him.

"Patsy and Liam were up at nine o'clock this morning, and he's got a gig tonight," he said, a little concerned. "It's going to be a monumental gig. It's going out to 300 million people, and he was still up at nine o'clock this morning with her.... so she's hardly a steadying influence is she? But yeah, they got engaged. I was like, 'What for?' He's going, 'Cos I loov 'er!' I'm like, I love her too man, but ... He's like, 'You should get engaged, man, it's top!' I'm like 'Fuck off!' I've got enough on my plate without having a fiancée to deal with.

"Am I gonna be married with children? No, no... Meg's always going on about it, when she's on the gin and tonics and that. 'Why won't you marry me, you bastard!' The way I see it, it's like, 'I'm already married to you, and it's not as if I'm going to fucking leave you.' If you wanna prance around in a fucking white dress, I'll buy you the dress. But I'm not going through a big rock'n'roll wedding. I've lived with her for two years now, so she's me common-law wife, so... Why spend ten grand on a wedding, when you can spend ten grand on a car?

"Or a guitar, even?"

Less than a year later and Noel would be eating his words. Liam and Patsy finally got married in a top secret ceremony in the first half of 1997. Initially everyone was alerted to a date which turned out to be false, thanks to tabloid and television reporting. Peggy Gallagher was transported down to London and preparations for

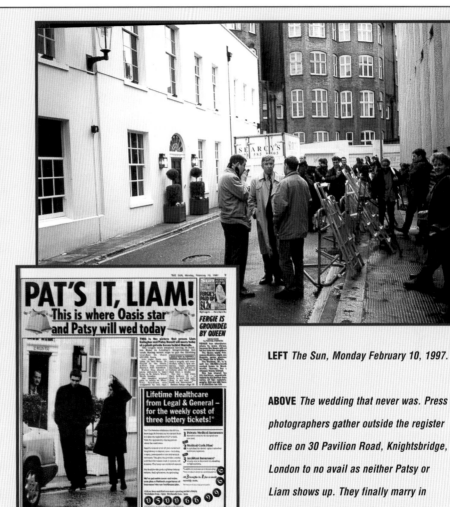

LEFT *The Sun, Monday February 10, 1997.*

ABOVE *The wedding that never was. Press photographers gather outside the register office on 30 Pavilion Road, Knightsbridge, London to no avail as neither Patsy or Liam shows up. They finally marry in secret at the Marylebone register office.*

a reception were being carried out at a top metropolitan club, but in the end the pair didn't go through with it — no doubt because the secret wasn't secret anymore. When they did finally marry, it was a very hushed up affair.

As for Noel, he eventually married Meg in the early summer of 1997, just a few months after his brother married Patsy. On June 1st, the *News Of The World* reported on his purchase of a mansion worth two million pounds in Buckinghamshire, and shortly afterwards he and Meg became husband and wife.

Their house was set on eight acres of property, was 100 years old, and contained eight bedrooms, a swimming pool, a snooker room, a tennis court and stables.

The summer of '97 reached a peak for Oasis with the release of their new single and album. "D' You Know What I Mean?" was released on 7 July 1997 and included a cover of David Bowie's "Heroes". On 17 July they appeared on *Top of the Pops*.

"D' You Know What I Mean?" was the fastest-selling single in the UK so far in 1997, with sales of 492,000 in just a two-week period. Disappointingly, however, Oasis were knocked off the Number One spot by Puff Daddy and Faith Evans' "I'll be Missing You", which, funnily, enough, Oasis had already toppled.

ABOVE *News of the World, Sunday June 1, 1997.*

There was amusement in the press when the *Daily Star* reported that the album *Be Here Now* was scheduled for release on Friday 18 July, marking the event with an eight-page Oasis special, which included a track listing and marks out of ten. However, *Melody Maker* reported that nobody at the paper had even heard the album!

With both Gallagher brothers settled into married life and new homes, and the success of the new album, the future of Oasis might be somewhat calmer, although their relationship with each other will no doubt continue in its volatile fashion. Their career has been short, but incredibly eventful. Their phenomenal appeal lies in their anthemic tunes, their 'rags to riches' story, their lairy attitude and their down to earth Mancunian spirit mixed with all the glamour rock'n'roll has to offer. Some have written them off as little more than perpetrators of the trend for laddishness which swept across Britain with the publication of *Loaded* magazine during the early nineties. Others have been outraged and appalled by their brattish, brutish public face, their snotty behaviour, their arrogance and their outspokenness. But many many more have been inspired by Oasis' belief in themselves, their ability to break out of the traps laid down by Tory rule, their hedonistic love of life and their dedication to living it large. Their seemingly over-confident macho swagger, their talk of birds, booze and blow, reek of all mouth, no trousers, yet their real attraction lies in their awkward, emotionally non-committal, almost shy masculinity.

ABOVE & FOLLOWING PAGES *Oasis back in the US. This time in San Francisco to support U2 on their POP MART tour.*

LEFT *Oasis begin shooting videos for their third LP, Be Here Now, at Stocks Country Club.*

Oasis have never sung about love and sex and broken hearts (even 'Wonderwall' wasn't that obvious), they maintain a cool, immobile stance onstage which acts as a barrier almost, a kind of anti-expression expression, and while essentially they are a man's band, women love them – and not just because of Liam's eyebrows. Their power is on the one hand very easily accessed, very simple, very straightforward, and on the other it's incredibly curious, relying on dynamics which seem to contradict each other, but obviously work perfectly together.

Unquestionably, the decade belongs to them. The world lies in the palm of their hands. Holding The Beatles up as a guide for their ambition (otherwise you might as well forget it, Noel once said), Oasis have declared that after their third album, their future is anyone's guess, although somehow it seems doubtful that rock music will ever be free from the Gallagher name. Maybe they'll self-combust, maybe they'll stick around until they're 50. Whatever they do, the likelihood is that no one will forget them.

LEFT *Another Rock 'n' Roll cliché, a Rolls Royce in a swimming pool. Be Here Now video shoot.*

THE NORTH'S NO.1
USINESS EQUIPMENT
SPECIALISTS

F.H.BROW

Oasis fans chase tour tickets

Oasis fans preparing for an overnight wait in Sheffield yesterday for tickets for the band's 13-date nationwide tour which go on sale this morning. The scene was repeated at tour venues in London, Aberdeen, Birmingham, Newcastle and Exeter, where fans slept rough overnight. A free phone line — 0800 1383333 — has been set up for fans to book the 156,000 tickets for the September tour. With only a limited number available from box offices, telephone operators are braced for a flood of calls and 300 telephone lines will open today to sell the bulk of the tickets. BT and Torch Telecom have been liaising for several weeks to ensure that the national network can cope with the expected demand. The band's record label, Creation, estimates that tickets will sell out by this evening. They will cost £17.50, or £19 for the three shows in London, plus a £1.50 booking charge.

ABOVE *The Times, Saturday July 26, 1997. Tickets go on sale and sell out for three shows at Londons Earls Court for the following September.*

LEFT *Liam models the new Manchester City strip on Maine Road turf.*

liam

noel

bonehead

guigs

alan